Let's Look at Life Cycles

A Frog's Life Cycle

Ruth Thomson

PowerKiDS press.

New York

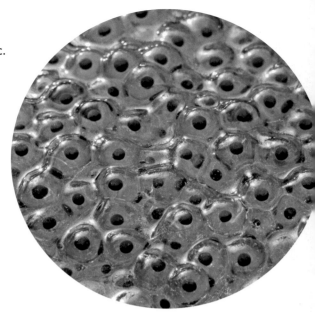

Published in 2010 by The Rosen Publishing Group Inc.
29 East 21st Street, New York, NY 10010

Copyright © 2010 Wayland/
The Rosen Publishing Group, Inc.

First Edition

Managing Editor: Victoria Brooker
Concept Designer: Paul Cherrill

Library of Congress Cataloging-in-Publication Data

Thomson, Ruth, 1949-
  A frog's life cycle / Ruth Thomson.
      p. cm. -- (Let's look at life cycles)
  Includes index.
  ISBN 978-1-61532-218-3 (library binding)
  ISBN 978-1-61532-224-4 (pbk.)
  ISBN 978-1-61532-225-1 (6-pack)
  1. Frogs--Life cycles--Juvenile literature. I. Title.
  QL668.E2T457 2010
  597.8'9--dc22
                                    2009023882

Photographs:
Cover, 15, 16 Robert Pickett/Papilio; 2, 12, 13, 14, 17, 18, 19 Photolibrary group; 4/5: Ian West/ Photolibrary Group; 6 Imagebroker/Photolibrary Group; 7, 9, 22 NHPA/Photoshot; 8 © Jean Hall/Cordaiy Photo Library Ltd./CORBIS; 10 London Scientific Films/Photolibrary Group; 11 David Boag/Photolibrary Group; 21 Woodfall/Photoshot

Manufactured in China

CPSIA Compliance Information: Batch #WAW0102PK: For Further Information

contact Rosen Publishing, New York, New York at 1-800-237-9932

Web Sites

Due to the changing nature of Internet links, PowerKids Press has developed an online list of Web sites related to the subject of this book. This site is updated regularly. Please use this link to access this list:
http://www.powerkidslinks.com/lllc/frog/

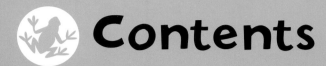# Contents

Frogs gather

It is springtime. Frogs gather at the pond where they were born.

How many frogs can you find?

The pond is a noisy place.
The male frogs croak
to attract a female.

Frogspawn

Each male sits on a female's back and grips her tight. She lays hundreds of eggs, which he covers with a liquid from his body.

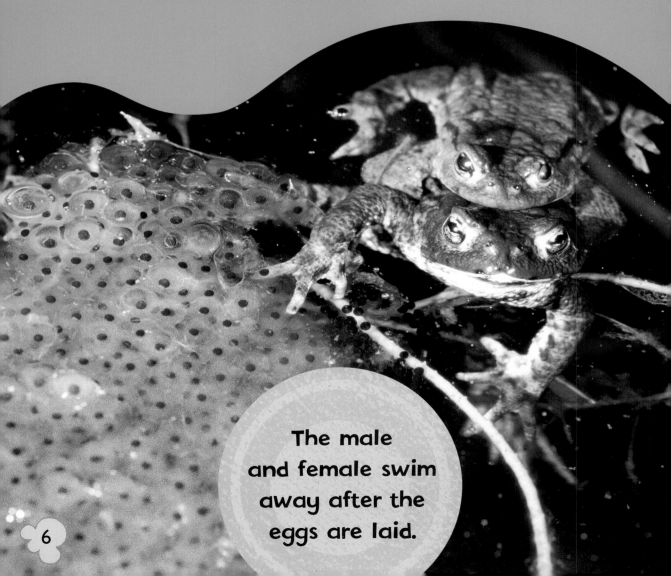

The male and female swim away after the eggs are laid.

Each egg is safe inside a clear jelly ball. The eggs stick together in a group called frogspawn. They float on top of the pond.

jelly

egg

Each jelly ball is the size of a pea.

Time to hatch

The eggs change shape. They grow longer. After about ten days, they become tadpoles.

Can you see both the tadpoles' head and tail?

The tadpoles begin to hatch.
They wriggle out of their jelly ball.
Then they stay together,
resting on the jelly.

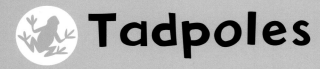# Tadpoles

Young tadpoles nibble tiny plants.
They breathe with the feathery gills
on each side of their heads.

2
weeks

The tadpoles grow longer.
Their feathery gills disappear.
They breathe with gills inside
their body instead.

How does a tadpole swim?

 # Food

As tadpoles grow, they start eating tiny flies and water fleas. Tadpoles eat dead worms and fish, too.

4 weeks

These tadpoles are sharing a dead worm.

Fish and bigger insects, like this dragonfly larva, eat the tadpoles.

Legs grow

The tadpole grows long back legs.
Its feet are webbed.

7 weeks

Why are webbed feet good for swimming?

14

Two shorter front legs grow.
The tadpole grows lungs instead
of gills. It comes to the surface
of the pond to breathe air.

9
weeks

 # Froglet

The tadpole's tail shortens.

Its eyes bulge. Its mouth widens.

It grows a tongue. It is now a froglet.

12 weeks

Soon, the froglet's tail will disappear. The froglet climbs out of the pond.

15 weeks

Fish, snakes, and birds eat tiny frogs.

Frog

The froglet slowly becomes an adult frog. It lives in damp places. Its blotchy skin makes it hard to see. It eats insects, worms, slugs, and spiders.

What is this frog eating?

The frog jumps from place to place
on its long back legs. It may dive
into the pond to escape hungry birds
and grass snakes that want to eat it.

Winter and spring

A frog cannot keep warm in cold weather.
It finds a safe hiding place for the winter.
It goes into a deep sleep called hibernation.

A frog does
not eat or
drink during
hibernation.

When frogs are two years old,
they are ready to find a mate. In the
spring, they go back to their pond.

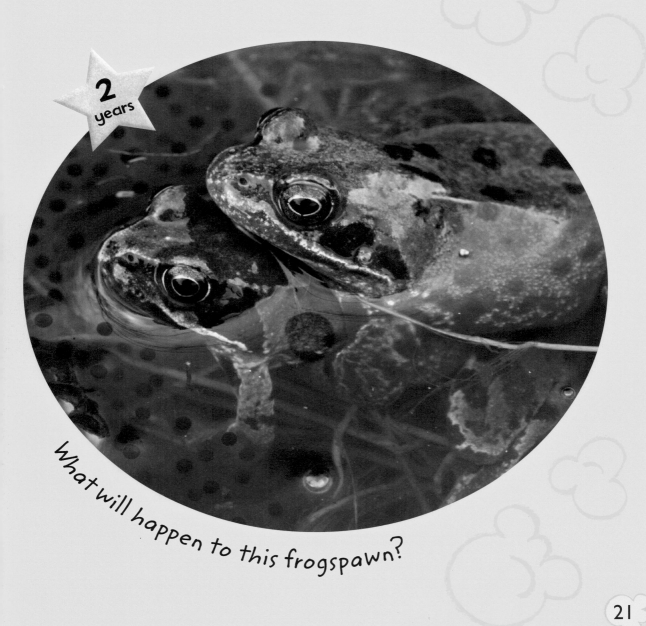

2 years

What will happen to this frogspawn?

Frog life cycle

In the spring, female frogs lay frogspawn. The frogspawn grows into tadpoles. The tadpoles become froglets and froglets become frogs.

frogspawn
Female frogs lay eggs
called frogspawn.

tadpole
Each egg hatches
into a tadpole.

frog
The froglet becomes a frog.

froglet
The tadpole grows back legs then front
legs and becomes a froglet.

Make a pop-up card

You will need:
- sheet of paper
- scissors
- crayons or felt-tip pens

Make a funny pop-up frog card to surprise a friend or someone in your family.

1. Fold the paper in half widthwise to make a crease. Open it out. Now fold it in half lengthwise.

2. Cut a slit through the folded paper beneath the crease, as shown.

3. Bend both corners of the slit into triangles.

4. Fold the paper into a greeting card.

5. Draw grass on the front.

Who is hiding in the grass?

6. Draw a big frog face inside, with the creased slit as its mouth.

Glossary and Further Information

croak to make a deep, harsh sound

female a girl frog

gills part that a tadpole uses to breathe underwater

hatch to come out of an egg

larva an insect in its first stage after hatching

lungs part of the body that animals use to breathe air

male a boy frog

mate the male or female partner of an animal

webbed feet feet with skin stretched between the toes

Books

The Life Cycle of a Frog
by Bobbie Kalman
(Crabtree Publishing Company, 2006)

The Life Cycle of a Frog
by Lisa Trumbauer
(Capstone Press, 2003)

The Life Cycle of a Frog
by Ruth Thomson
(PowerKids Press, 2007)

Index